COMETOLOGY

poems by

STEPHEN BROCKWELL

MISFIT   ECW PRESS

NATIONAL LIBRARY OF CANADA CATALOGUING IN PUBLICATION DATA

Brockwell, Stephen
Cometology

"A misfit book."

ISBN 1-55022-451-4

1. Title.

PS8553.R6135C65 2001   C811'.54   C00-933256-1
PR9199.3.B76C65 2001

Edited by Michael Holmes / a misFit book
Cover and text design by Tania Craan
Cover photo by Jack Zehrt / FPG Canada Inc.
Text images by Marc Gauthier and Dan Marion
Author photo copyright studio von dulong
Layout by Mary Bowness

Printed by AGMV

Distributed in Canada by
General Distribution Services,
325 Humber College Blvd.,
Toronto, ON M9W 7C3

Published by ECW PRESS
2120 Queen Street East, Suite 200
Toronto, ON M4E 1E2
ecwpress.com

This book is set in Futura and Garamond.

PRINTED AND BOUND IN CANADA

The publication of *Cometology* has been generously supported by the Canada Council, the Ontario Arts Council and the Government of Canada through the Book Publishing Industry Development Program.
Canadä

ACKNOWLEDGEMENTS

I owe a significant poetic debt to Peter van Toorn, Endré Farkas, and Ken Norris, who published my first work and included some of these poems in the anthology *Sounds New* (Muses' Company, 1990). This is the first payment, long overdue.

Kind thanks to David Solway, Michael Harris, David McGimpsey, rob mclennan, Susan McMaster, Ronnie Brown, Diana Brebner, Adrienne Ho, Jeffrey Donaldson, Marc Gauthier, and Michael Holmes, who in small or large ways nurtured these poems.

I would like to acknowledge the editors of *The Antigonish Review, Arc, bluemoon, Descant, Open Set* (Agawa Press, 1990), *Prism International, Yak, Zymergy, It's Still Winter,* and *Poets 88* (Quarry Press, 1988) where a number of these poems first appeared.

The technical drawings in "Constructive Geometry" are reproduced from *Differential Geometry of Curves and Surfaces,* by Manfredo P. Do Carmo with kind permission of Prentice Hall.

This book is dedicated to Nicole, Danica, and Mathieu, who have put up with my obsession, and to my mother, who has endured suffering.

CONTENTS

BETELGEUSE

1

A boy stands in the rain forest
looking through a hole in the canopy
at Betelgeuse: the shoulder of the hero.

He stares at the star. His feet
grip the forest floor. The tips of the vines
grow through the tender soles of his feet,

follow his blood through his veins.
He embraces the numbness and nausea
of an earthly epiphany.

He watches the stars until dawn
and moves to go. A vine in his tongue
makes song from his breathing.

2

A miner on the edge of the rain forest
sees the image of a face
in petrified wood.

His crew saws a slab from the rock
that he takes home. He polishes the slab
for hours and designs iron legs for a garden table.

He has the legs cast at the foundry.
Iron ivy curls around them, he praises
the blacksmith's skill.

That night he stands a telescope on the slab,
searching the mirror through the polished lens
for Betelgeuse.

COMETOLOGY

When beggars die there are no comets seen:
The heavens themselves blaze forth the death of princes.
— William Shakespeare, *Julius Caesar*

As it hovered over Jesus
Painted by Giotto in His beastly
Manger.
                    How many heralds blasted
A fanfare across the skies, some
Lies, some otherwise.
                    I sit and listen. Scientists probe
How many ions make its tail
Ten million astronomical
Units outward.
            — Ralph Gustafson, "Ions One-Thousandth the
            Width of a Pinhead"

EPISODES

1986

The steel, burning cabin
of the shuttle Challenger
explodes into the Atlantic.
The faint tail of Halley disappoints
a face behind binoculars.

Opening the door to her daughter's
bedroom, Mrs. Allison finds
two moving naked bodies,
closes the door, never
speaks of it.

1910

In the Oklahoma hills
Select Followers offer a young girl
to the feathered star.
Alerted by a suspicious farmer,
police arrive before she dies.

Driving for the first time,
Mike O'Neil raises dust.
Distracted by the comet,
he avoids a bewildered dog, crushes
the grille on the trunk of an elm.

1833

Osceola, chief of the Seminoles,
carver of treaties, carver of scalps,
after the passage of a comet
and an order of expulsion
massacres a settlement.

Beating dust from the sheets
with a broom, Anne
glimpses a comet over the roof.
The doorstep delivers a lost letter
from her husband, four months dead.

RECENT DISCOVERIES

Tungsten is a filament of wire
not the source of the light
beside the bed in the child's room.
A current heats the wire,
heat illuminates the coil.
After a thousand hours, the coil breaks
as a comet, eroded by the solar wind,
shatters in its last orbit;
each fragment becomes a new comet
orbiting the sun.
What shape of your head
should we most fear?
Aster pitheus: the jar-shaped star
pours stones of the Aquarid
meteor showers across the Earth's path,
a bearer of water
in a dust-covered urn
feared as the vessel
for a fatal epidemic.
Aster ceratias: the horned star
scores the surface of the moon
like a territorial ram,
seldom promises fortune,
a mocking cornucopia.
Aster argenteo: the silver star
is formed of a perishable,
semi-precious metal,
its lustre diminishes
in the absence of the Sun.

Is your anti-tail a speechless
tongue? You are Lyttleton's flying sand-dune,
accreted interstellar dust.
You are Whipple's dirty snowball,
primordial water and stone.
These are the tools of your study:
dust mass spectrometer,
multicolour camera,
radio telescope,
magnetometer,
binoculars,
contact lens,
eye.

EPISODES

1597

As her ships prepare for open sea,
Elizabeth casts
a defiant eye
at the comet, a dire portent
feared by her advisors.

Alone with her son
without peat,
midwinter in Donegal,
a carpenter's wife burns
the legs of the oak table.

1572

A comet is taken
as a sign of wrath
after the late-summer
slaughter
of St Bartholomew's Huguenots.

Madeleine,
thirty years old,
abused by her husband
for not bearing a child,
bears a bastard son.

1337

A comet's slow procession
over London
precedes the passage of carts
carrying the bodies of dozens
dead from the Black plague.

Marion prays
for the life of her fever-held
daughter. The night her daughter
dies, Marion conceives
under her husband's shoulder.

CLASSICAL OBSERVATIONS

Candle wax is a secretion from the bee
not the source of the wavering
light above the astrologer's desk.
Fingers carry an ember,
a dry wick catches the spark
as a passing solar system
disturbs a body from the cloud
of sleeping ice and stone
at the limit of the Sun's influence.
A comet begins the long elliptical fall
to graze the Sun's surface,
to gather a coma and tail
from the solar wind and magnetic field.
What shape of your tail
should we most fear?
Aster acontiea: the spear star,
thrown at the sun
from an unknown arm,
deflected by accident
of orbit, devastates
a remote Siberian forest.
Aster lampadias: the torch star
illuminates a cavern
without walls, where no hand
has painted an image of the hunt;
its light reflects
from the thin steel surface
of the satellite Giotto.
Aster xiphias: the dagger star,

polished by the solar wind,
carves flesh from a distance,
ubiquitous at deaths
of ancient kings.
Is your coma a veil that hides
a dull face of rock and ice?
You are Kepler's stellar arrows,
never returning.
You are Halley's periodic orbiter,
the Sun's kite.
These are the tools of your study:
astrolabe, gnomon,
telescope,
torquetum,
baculus,
eye.

EPISODES

1066

On the Bayeux tapestry:
a small sky-axe
woven above Harold's
crown at Hastings.
They were in awe of the star.

After a bitter winter,
a farmer's son
ploughs from the muddy furrows
his father's gold cross
thought stolen the previous year.

CA. 4 B.C.

Instructed that a comet
foretold the birth
of a greater King, Herod
kills a generation of Judean
sons, cuts off his youngest heirs.

In an Armenian forest, a boy
kills his first wild boar.
His father rewards him
with a new bow
and an unknown woman's arms.

CA. 1000 B.C.

King Wu marches on Zhou,
faces east. After a flood
Gongtou falls. A comet appears;
the dagger's handle
points to the people of Yin.

Pi Li, six years old,
catches a yellow butterfly
the size of her hands,
carries its wing-dust
all day in her palms.

EARLY BELIEFS

Flint is a black stone
not the source of the fire
beneath the roasting hare.
Striking the stone causes fire
as a meteor carves
light from the outer atmosphere,
as the solar wind
fans the peacock feathers
of a comet's tail.
What shape of your head
should we most fear?
Aster hircus: the goat star
seems almost to have a human
fallen face
with horns and coarse hair,
tail perpetually erect,
goat's beard long, white
threads between the planets.
Aster pogonius: the beard star,
red-coiled with rage,
captures light
like beads of saliva,
or hangs gently, the fine
threads on the rice-paper skin
of an old man walking in the garden.
Aster hippeus: the horse star
flays the solar wind with its tail;
it was not recognized as rock and ice
but as a serpent of the atmosphere

as we once believed wild horses
were serpents of the field.
Is your tail an arm
stretched to regain the momentum
of falling to perihelion,
because you fear aphelion,
the return to darkness
and the loss of speed?
You are Seneca's eccentric
celestial body.
You are Aristotle's fiery principle,
an exhalation among the vapours.
These are the tools of your study:
water clock,
sundial,
eye.

NOTES FROM SLEEP

At times we will have to howl with the wolves, and that means that we will have to forget some things that are familiar, especially those things that prevent us from understanding strange contents.
— Hans Peter Duerr, *Dreamtime*

Que tu viennes du ciel ou de l'enfer, qu'importe,
O Beauté! monstre énorme, effrayant, ingénu!
— Charles Beaudelaire, "Hymne à la Beauté"

WHITE NOISE

Listen to the static on the radio.
You can hear laughter, excited cries, barking dogs.
Watch white noise on the television.
The people of the white noise make love,
the white dogs stand watch.
The random noise of sleep
awakens me and I record it.
Or, I step into a memory,
the first sheet of November ice.
I try to jot notes down but
the memory is distorted as I write.
I have to be at work in half an hour.
I hear the bus down the street.
An ending, an image, is lost in illegible
transcription as I walk out the door without my keys.

MOTH GLITTER

Walk naked downstairs at 3 in the morning
into an unfinished kitchen extension.
Suspended from the ceiling on a blue
cable, a bulb burns, drawn to the mirror
of your body. Bathe in that light. Outside,
moths are gathering on the incomplete,
plastic covered windows. Patience. The moths
see two sources of light: the unbearably
bright burning fist of the bulb and the long
comfortable bed of light reflecting
from your body. A moth will find a gap
to crawl through. You will hear fluttering wings
close to your ear. The shadow of the moth
will cast its inverted star on the bare floor.
If you walk slowly to the stairs, the moth
will follow, dropping on your skin like rain.
If you rush up to bed and lie on the sheet
the moth will find the glow of your warm skin
and splash your thighs with its wings. If you can
rest there until morning while the moth wings
fall like a sable brush on your body
illegibly painted with moth glitter,
you will know how to fly in Apple Hill
and how to raise the dead in Pointe-aux-Trembles.

WAKING DREAM

Belly full of seafood, I parked the station-wagon in front of the garage and entered the farmhouse by the back door. It was late and overcast. I couldn't see the staircase that led from the back shed into the kitchen. I thought I heard a cat on the woodpile. I edged my feet forward, feeling for the steps, and found the cold surface of the metal door. One foot on the bottom step, I groped for the doorknob. A red glow filled the door. Dark images of people danced on a carpet of fire. A burning face greeted me with a peculiar, knowing grin. A cat ran between my legs. I opened the door, perspiring slightly. My father sat under the bright light of the kitchen table feeding the thick tobacco smoke that hovered above his head.

A BULL AT THE CATTLE SHOW

People encircle the pen of the charolais bull
to admire the girth of his testicles.
The cattle-hall ceilings are church high.
Flakes of blue paint drop from the walls;
light from the dust-covered windows is dim.
The floor is of straw and manure-covered boards.
Pine plank fences of various dimensions
make a maze of the cattle-hall.
A young boy jeers at the bull,
teases with a straw shaft.
The charolais bull escapes,
shatters the pen, charges through people
who leap over boards, jump through windows
to escape the pummelling hooves.
Through the wood and glass of a door
the bull runs free to the street
head rolling on its shoulders,
a hooked marlin over water,
collides with a passing truck,
falls slowly, head
rolling. Steam rises from the crushed
red hood and radiator of the truck.
People gather, shocked by oil pools in the blood.

LEANING TREES

I pull her hand up the mountain.
Red and orange leaves blanket the ground.
Trees tilt downhill.
Near the summit, three shapes of men
stand in the sun. Her breasts touch my back.
If these men don't leave, we won't make love.
As we approach, they run downhill toward the sea.
Their leather jerkins blend into forest.
I look in the sun's direction.
Her hand is in mine, but I'm afraid to turn.
The sea shimmers, a shaken blanket.
Colours appear repeatedly in the sea:
orange, blue; orange, white.
Her breasts touch my back.
I recognize the hardness of her nipples.

SUPPER

A head of goat, head of lamb, and leg of beef
fill a plate with dark liquid.
The tablecloth is yellowing white lace;
I recognize faces in the ornate patterns.
The oak table has a wax coating;
I furrow the wax with my thumbnail.
White cloth on his arm, a servant clears the table.
The leg of beef kicks. Eyes in the goat's head
open to the servant, turn to me.
I stand under a plane tree.
A colourful tribe chants and dances.
Yellow and blue spikes in their head-dresses
rise and fall with the rhythm of the dance.
We herd water buffalo to a riverbank.
I fire a long rifle. The tribe throws spears.
Buffalo fall to water, hewn logs.
Look down at the water:
their eyes turn in their sockets.

A BRIDGE INTERRUPTED

Barefoot on gravel, I pass thatch-roofed houses.
Grey moss hangs from the eaves.
Wind sings through the broken glass;
the doors slap their frames in undanceable rhythms,
brass hinges are oxidized piccolos.
A boy follows closely,
blue-striped white shirt exposing his navel,
hands clasped in front of him.
The gravel ends at a shoreline.
A truncated bridge spans half the lake,
interrupted oak planks are suspended over the water,
the iron railings are unbolted.
Stacked slabs of stone rise from the middle of the lake.
I swim among sunfish and luminescent flora.
A water-image of my thighs
darkens the stone table where the slabs are stacked.
Beetles commute between crevices.
Near my hand, a frog: still, jade.
Spheres cover its head, discarded
imperfect emeralds.
From the bridge, the boy looks down
where I tread water, sees his face
reflected in each facet of the waves.

FLIES IN THE HEAT

Heat catalyses an organic
process on the manure pile:
gold flies cluster on the heap
of straw and excrement, cloud
the air around the pile in slow diffusion.
Cattle in the field are nervous.
A visiting farmer approaches the pile,
stops before entering the expanding
sphere of flies, hears
the electrical hum of wings.
Helical swarms embalm him,
construct a honey-coloured exoskeleton.
Amber needles, his legs compass
closer to the pile;
he's lost in the growing swarm of flies.
Cattle surround the pond
at the field's edge.
At the limit of their diffusion,
the flies are too sparse to see.

LUNAR OBSERVATORY

Rings of Jupiter. Fury
of the red storm. Titan's bursts:
frozen gas. Orion. Ursa Major.
Across the room, naked,
completely self-composed,
she watches stars. I will not
catalogue her beauty.
She is Renoir she is Turner she is Verdi.
Words come effortlessly to her.
But tired of conversation,
she studies the sky. From hip to thigh
a birthmark: dark skin,
roughened. Between her legs
an excess of flesh.
Vulva   testicle   vestige of birth
I adore her ambiguity.

WHALE TEETH

Embraced by warm ocean, shore invisible,
the emerald depths of water clear:
vegetation on the ocean floor
sways in the current of a whale's flukes.
I rise in the swell of its careless swimming,
from neck to navel rise with the water,
limbs pulling at the waves for shore.
In the rounded ivory of a whale's teeth
my ankles are pinned.
Pushed to air, I see the reef below me
as I fall in a parabola to water.
Clasped again, tossed into foam
and again.
Terror dissipating,
I watch their grey enamel backs
from the reef of waist-deep coral.

A SWAMP EXPERIENCE

A holstein cow floats by the kitchen window.
The sun rises, an orange and grey sky
reflects from the white spots on the cow.
The cow floats over electric wires.
I run after it on a tubular gravel road;
poplar leaves shimmer green on both sides.
At the end of the road, stands the fattest man I've seen,
lumberjack shirt-sleeves rolled up, wrists white slugs.
He shows me his house, gives me tea.
Sunlight and cedar panelling in every room,
old bronze guns on the wall.
He shows me his back yard.
Silt pools cover his lawn, the pores of a face.
His wife looks at us, peculiar.
We put on thick rubber boots, rubber jackets.
The boots reach my groin.
He leads me to the swamp
where the cow floats over the bulrushes.
I step in and sink in water to my chin.

FARM ANIMALS

Head to palms, in a house no longer his,
the farmer expects an electrical storm.
His wife accuses him, eyes on the field.
In the shed, he searches for a carpenter's tool.
Azure clouds at dusk. Auras from hydro lines:
transformers emit thick knots of light,
layers of blue neon, rhythmic
surges of humming, the scent of ionized gas.
Tubes of light encase wires near the barn.
Entering, a child stops on the doorsill.
A blue sheet of light descends,
covers the motionless child.
A dog from the shed doorway
limps to the yard, carries a cloud of light;
disoriented, it convulses,
yaps in confusion, rolls in grass and air
without sense of ground.
The farmer, in tears, carries a gun he fears to raise.
The dog runs into a fence, cuts its paws,
traps its head. Still at the crack of a gun.
Fur of white fire, a cat walks in circles,
unbalanced, cries muted by surges of humming.
Still at the crack of a gun.
A bird from a wire flies to the ground,
still in a pool of light.
In the field, holding the wife's gaze,
a mountain under a falling cloud of light,
the bull kicks earth and grass,
crawls under a sheet of light,
falls on its ribs. Fence posts

snap under its weight.
Still at the crack of a gun.
A full moon visibly falls. Clouds of dust
conduct light across the fields.
A child in a doorway.
A two-storey train passes in the distance.
Each illuminated window
reveals the eyes of a curious face.

A CRACKED CUP

I warm tea in a birthday gift cup
directly on the burner.
The cup cracks, steam
rises from the stove;
from the crack, I sip
the last mouthful of remaining tea.
In the living room, fade
photographs of old friends,
dulled black and white,
sepia tinted light blue. The corners
of the photographs are smeared.
Sunlight projects lace shadows
through the curtains.
The carpet seems never to have been
walked on. In one frame
above the fireplace,
unrecognizeable eyes.

THE SOW

The prize sow is restless when I enter the garage.
Seven piglets at her teats, her head sways, distrustful.
The sow rises, runs around the garage;
piglets fall, hooves slide on concrete,
her back legs slide under her.
A hip dislocates from its socket.
She runs, half-crippled. Fallen around her,
the piglets squeal, reach for her teats.
Father sees the dislocated hip,
pulls the sow down by her neck,
holds her head to the floor, sends me for an axe.
I circle the garage; searching,
find only a hammer he makes me bring.

TAUNTING THE BOAR

On the earth above the high lagoon bank,
children watch swimming sharks.
I swim toward them, brushed by a shark's cold leather.
The water level is low.
Logs and grey rocks span the river bottom,
a ribcage covered by silt.
Alan stands among the silent children,
leads me to a plain of dry grass
and scattered, grey-leafed deciduous trees.
A herd of wild pigs, cattle-sized,
grazes in circular array, hairless, dark purple.
Alan taunts a boar on the perimeter
with unintelligible sounds.
The glistening boar charges.
We run to a tree where a dust-caked blanket hangs,
long tusks in pursuit.
Around and around, hidden by the blanket,
we run until the boar drops exhausted, a pearl in dust.
We watch its lungs rise and fall while it sleeps.

HONEY JAR

Trunk wider than a bear,
limbs gnarled, grey coral.
On the trunk, a lip of bark
consumes a strand of barbed wire.
The wire was clipped to save the fence.
Rot begins its slow digestion;
pungent sap drips from the tree,
flows in volume,
gases and heat stream from the lip.
Wood behind the trunk
appears. Mutable colours
permeate the grain:
aquamarine, garnet.
A jar of liquefied honey falls
from underneath the lip of bark.
The carcasses of flies
are suspended in the jar,
preserved, delectable fruit.

FOG ON THE MOOR

On a green hill we stand naked in fog
in a ring of cedars and silver birch.
Her hair shines with the dampness of fog,
the skin of her breasts smooth with dew
near the outline of her ribs.
Her labia are extended, could engulf me.
She moves the sole of one foot
over the top of the grass.
I fail to watch without reverence.

A CHRISTMAS UKULELE

Grandmother sits
smiling beside a bottle of gin.
I hold the grey wrapping paper
from her gift. A cardboard
violin and ukulele are packed in a shoe box
with thinly shredded newspaper.
Surprisingly, the neck of the violin
doesn't bend in my hand.
I draw the paper bow across it.
Sounds escape. Not the sounds
of a violin.
I rummage through boxes for the real violin —
she must be teasing.
In the dining room,
bright wool yarmulke on his head,
Peter plays the ukulele.
The strings intersect over the sound box.
Each string he plays plays all the other strings.

BIRCH MESSAGES

To print this message on birch bark,
I walk east of Ottawa, in a forest
thick with cedars. Among fallen leaves,
half frozen in a pool, lies a racoon,
mouth open. Preserved in snow,
its tracks lead to a stand of silver
birch. A wild dog stalks
behind the birches,
revealing only fragments:
matted fur, a gaping jaw.
I fillet bark from a birch,
take this note.
I hear the dog breathe; its shape
spans trees, hunger in the hollow
fragments of its body. Snow falls,
covers my footprints; the racoon's
tracks are a memory.
I run between trees, hide behind
trunks, hear the dog's breath
following. Its four paws.
I look back from the verge
of the cedars; the dog
wanders on the edge of the forest,
tongue to the left, its breath a mist
preceding it. I watch its grey eyes
for a moment. Bored, the dog wanders
back among the trees, stitching
an angular path in fresh snow.

SALVE PODS

An ice water barrel contains
the crystal shapes of two human faces.
Water runs between layers of ice and skin,
a moving pattern of dark veins.
Clothed in mustard-coloured cotton,
a man and woman
carry pods of salve to the barrel
and place them on the glass ledge of the rim.
They step back. Arms break
from the surface of ice; fingertips
peel ice squares from each forehead.
Two hands of mosaic ice
apply the salves to exposed skin.
Beneath the ice: enigmatic
smiles beyond distinction,
rivulets of water.

WAKING DREAM

The bag lady sat outside on the sill of the only light-giving window of the basement apartment. I was spooning corn flakes into my mouth and listening to Handel. The darkness prompted me to play *Into Something* by Yussef Lateef. The bag lady was comfortably leaning on the windowsill. I sat and watched her fumble through her belongings. The room became completely dark. I stood in a long black plain. After walking for a time, I came to a precipice filled with undulating clouds of dust. Polished black spheres appeared in the dust and travelled on random trajectories. Occasionally, one would become buoyant and rise infinitely upward from the precipice or fall and permanently disappear in the dust. A last chorus of horns. A cat replaced the bag lady in the window.

AN ARTHRITIC SHOULDER

Suffer, she says. If you recognize her face as she lights
a cigarette on rue Drolet, do not fear to demand her
attention; cross the street and ask her for a kiss.
You may have the fortune to be
slapped by her irreverent hand.
A grandmother, in an alcoholic stupor, beats
the buttocks of her two-year-old grandson raw
with a brush. The boy will never remember the colour
of the bruises, the shape of the bristles, the aroma
of the breath — was it vodka, gin, or rum?
Suffer, he says. If he knocks, open the door.
He is an evangelist with an important message.
He will deliver pamphlets that burn in your hand.
With a smile, he will urge you to read them.
He will ask, *When will it be convenient to return?*
An uncle prods his niece. *Too fat! Not much
chance of getting laid with thighs like that. What's this?*
She has unspoken fears of basements,
bedrooms, men over thirty. She loves
chrysanthemums, azaleas, well fertilized soil.
Suffer, they say. *Suffer*. Tears brim her eyes.
He laughs. She grabs your tie and pulls it tightly
around your neck until you are choking. His teeth
and tongue flash; he is insulting you in a language
you cannot understand. After the first
penetration of the tongue, after the first
explosion of desire was tasted they fled
from life as dogs from thunder.
I have an arthritic condition of the shoulder;
I cherish each message from the nerve like a letter

from my father. A letter I never received
since he could not write. There is no madness
in this love of pain. We suffer too little.
The bone spurs on my shoulder are beautiful,
merciful, constant.

WINTER FIREFLIES

Static sparks raise my hair as I take off my shirt
in a dry electrically heated room.
The window creaks in a tide of wind and snow;
weather warnings are broadcast on the radio.
Only streetlights and trees waver in the wind.
Fishtailing around the corner, a car
skids off a patch of ice into the ditch.
The car door opens like a palpitating gill.
The driver emerges. Under the streetlight,
in a current of driving snow, flakes collect
on his hair and shoulders like particles of steel.
The flakes ignite as he lights a cigarette.
I will dress, go out, and help him move his car,
pushing through the white swarm of winter fireflies.

COMPULSIVE IN
THE PUBLIC LIBRARY

1

Card catalogue
the altar for this ceremony
this sacrifice of texts
hectic experiment of style and violence

The Minister of Compulsion
        Dustin Hoffman *Midnight Cowboy*
        long black wool coat
        dirty canvas shoes   no socks
        orange cotton pants   rolled cuffs
        a second pair underneath   eggshell blue
                operating room pants!
        white cotton shirt   cavalier sleeves
        black beard to his collar bone   threads of white
        dishevelled Gregory Peck
                Ahab of the wheel road
                searching for that bound leviathan
                a fat, defaceable book

2

Midnight Cowboy, a jaundiced industrial production,
the word-assassin mutters to himself

unfolds a blanket
          black and orange plaid
unwraps a headrest
          a tube   black rubber
          under the catalogue
locates the headrest
orients it with his right foot
          seeking perfect position
places the blanket on the seat
pulls the chair from the wall
opens the blanket on the chair
          bending twice: hip/knee
sits

3

These were his subjects:
        Hibbin, Sally, *The Official James Bond Movie Book*,
New York: Crown Publishers
        Ciment, Michel, *Kubrick*,
Paris (?): Calmann-Levy
        James, David E., *Allegories of Cinema*,
Princeton: Princeton University Press

A vandal's bibliography
to be taken up from the floor
by a spectator
who fails to intervene
not for fear of violence
but to perpetuate the experience

4

These words: the absence of light
Film,
a reflection of light project
-ed —
plot thought

Words, tired vessels for belief,
how poorly they stack up
against a photograph,
how they clog the present continuous of film:
projecting at sixty frames per second
a film is worth 432,000,000 words

5

Reflected from incandescent
overhead lights:
images from film — a fan's bric-a-brac
columns of words between stills,
prolix captions
reflected in the Minister's glasses:

Bond, priest of style and kitsch
        lethal elegance
                women are trained to love
        a single personality in multiple bodies,
        a comic hero scattered among the stars

Kubrick, producer philosopher,
        from *Spartacus* to *Odyssey*
        with budgets, accountants, staff
        like clockwork,
        has paid for his shining poetry

Brakhage, anonymous film
        maker, frame by frame
        cutting celluloid eyes
        light unmediated in
        films so rare
        we only read of them in books

6

The Minister of Compulsion
holds two steel ornaments —
jetliners —   from the hood of what old car?
        flies over the pages
                surveillance
                matching an image of woman
                        to a photograph from film
        flips through Kubrick, reduced to black and white
                removes a loose page
                        Clockwork Orange   a shaken lover
        skims *Allegories of Cinema*
                photographs of pornography art films
        reads Bond   on the frontispiece
                a woman wearing diamonds   evening, blue light
                diamonds on her hips   on her hands
                on her pistol

This is the site of his solitary violence and art

7

Reader, what do you see?
Please, write:

_____

_____

_____

_____

In this, at least,
participate:
if you will not write
then read

to intervene
in this parody of censorship
before the intent to damage
becomes the will to cut,
before the desire to erase
the permanent by-products of film
becomes an act,
a stack of pages pulled from a broken book

8

Thought in images:
countless
early reels of silent
captionless pornography:
instructions for possession
I own the image of your body
compliant, attentive
quiet
come, oddity

Thought in an image:
People of Sarawak
hide their eyes from your camera
primitives! Pfbbt!
Their soul in light
they may kill you for the camera,
ignorant censors
captured in a reel of documentary film

Thought in images:
8mm home movies:
swimming, Lac Nominingue
the swimmer   no longer swimmer
like the water in that lake
now cloud, fish, river, sea

scattered by thirty years of circulation

9

The Minister of Compulsion
places the texts on the card catalogue
grips the Official Bond text and Kubrick
a ballpoint pen   shirt pocket
a pair of scissors!
cuts a page from Kubrick
Barry Lyndon's youthful consort
draws on Bond
cuts a fine figure
          into the page

Never an expression

Police, quiet, respectful,
help him from the library
an embarrassed political Minister
snubbed for unconventional beliefs
and frequent indiscretions,
Minister of a portfolio
few consider glamorous

10

What messages did he transcribe
between photograph and word
to mark his reading?

An address:
curling gothic script
under a photograph: Grace Jones's
shin raised to a face
with a view to a kill

A circle around a weapon:
Scaramanga's cigarette lighter,
a disguised golden pistol
pressed to Andrea's cheek
A life in film:
the time to smoke a cigarette

A geometric spiral:
Bond poised to tackle
a midget wrestler in a tuxedo,
Mary Goodnight
wrapped modestly in sheets

He cut an X into the page
where Jill Masterson's pores
suffocate, painted gold
Background to the page: Bond's
bleeding pistol barrel,
rifling like a fossilized mollusc,
inspiration for his geometric spiral

CONSTRUCTIVE GEOMETRY

One can argue that a universe governed by laws that do not allow consciousness is no universe at all. I would even say that all the mathematical descriptions of a universe that have been given so far fail this criterion. It is only the phenomenon of consciousness that can conjure a putative 'theoretical' universe into actual existence!

    — Roger Penrose, *The Emperor's New Mind*

When Lampman maintains that the growth of the soul consists in each creature's following its own bent, he diametrically opposes the central impulse of his culture, which would change or transform life to make it fit some ideal pattern — which would impose an order upon life.

    — D. G. Jones, *Butterfly on Rock*

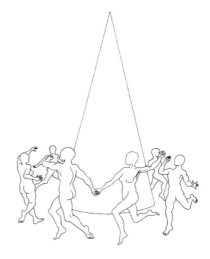

CONSTRUCTIVE GEOMETRY

Change
without difference:
homo erectus, engineer:
makers, a flint implement,
the Eiffel tower.
Movement
perceived as one thing:
the tide, a bird's flight,
a dance, an act of love.

You cannot build with your hands
all possible shapes
you can imagine.
You cannot imagine
all possible shapes.
Your hands are the limbs
of an age,

build with them:
with coloured paper
make a theatre
for foolscap dancers.
Bend this sheet,
a geometer's origami,

or with a Bunsen burner
and a palm of sand
shape with your hands
what cannot last:
this page,
your hands,
earth.

POINT

$x(u,v) = (a, b, c)$
A parameter-free representation of a point

Dim origin.
No matter how close
I place the eye,
represented by
the smallest dot.
No pin sharp enough
to push you.
No pen fine enough
to place you.
Take a pen, draw a point.
Take a pin, push it out.
Look through it.
When I draw the line
you can't be counted on:
everything to everyone —
yes, you take a position
but you carry no weight.

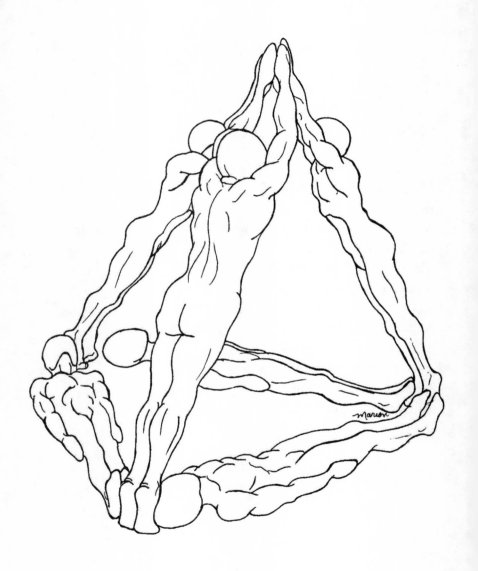

TETRAHEDRON

$x(u,v) = (u, v, 0)$ for $\{(u,v);\ 0 \leq u + v \leq 1\} \cup$
$(u, 0, v)$ for $\{(u,v);\ 0 \leq u + v \leq 1\} \cup$
$(0, u, v)$ for $\{(u,v);\ 0 \leq u + v \leq 1\} \cup$
$(u, v, 1 - u - v)$ for $\{(u,v);\ 0 \leq u + v \leq 1\}$
Parametric representations of four triangles forming a tetrahedron

First solid, deviant pyramid:
no platform for a tomb
no capsule for the luminous eye.
At the airport
fold three newspapers
corner to corner,
staple the long edges
constructing a hat.
Wear it.
Collect the anxiety
of curious passengers,
become an artesian well
for their asymmetrical energy.
You are a primitive
for ailerons and turbofans.
Fly.

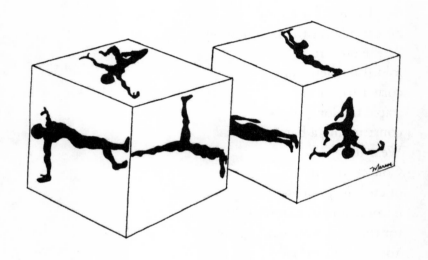

CUBE

$x(u,v) = (u, v, 1)$ for $\{(u,v);\ 0 \le u \le 1, 0 \le v \le 1\}\ \cup$

$(u, 1\ v)$ for $\{(u,v);\ 0 \le u \le 1, 0 \le v \le 1\}\ \cup$

$(1, u, v)$ for $\{(u,v);\ 0 \le u \le 1, 0 \le v \le 1\}\ \cup$

$(u, v, 0)$ for $\{(u,v);\ 0 \le u \le 1, 0 \le v \le 1\}\ \cup$

$(u, 0, v)$ for $\{(u,v);\ 0 \le u \le 1, 0 \le v \le 1\}\ \cup$

$(0, u, v)$ for $\{(u,v);\ 0 \le u \le 1, 0 \le v \le 1\}$

Parametric representations of the unit squares composing a unit cube

Die
rolled in the corner
of a shanty house
a rat crawls
in your edges of dirt.
Tête carré,
your faces
are the walls of a cell.
In a classroom,
four walls of red brick,
a young girl's letter blocks
spell
CAT.

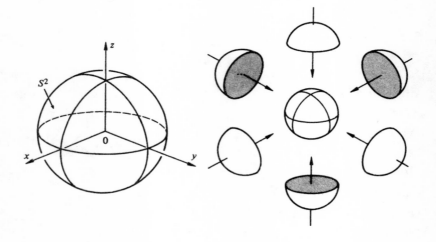

SPHERE

x(u,v) = (sin u cos v, sin u sin v, cos v) for {(u,v); 0 < u < π, 0 < v < 2π}
A parameterization for one of the six hemispheres that cover the unit sphere

A bearing:
womb on the last day.
Ball-bearing
of the greased wheel:
more than pumpkin-hard.
The rigidity of the sphere:
a soap-bubble
in a child's hand.
In a child's hand
a basketball deforms,
becomes projectile,
gathers momentum,
fragments the skull.
The rigidity of the sphere.
Still, open eyes:
a bearing.

MONKEY SADDLE

$x(u,v) = (u,\ v,\ u^3 - 3v^2u)$

A parametric representation of the monkey saddle

This sheet at three
corners held.
A man with three legs
would strap you
to a two-headed horse.
The surface of the grass
in a three mountain valley.
The surface of the snow
in a three valley mountain.
Be comforted:
a linen sheet
at the head of a bed,
edge held in small hands;
at the foot of a bed
in a mother's hands,
two corners falling.

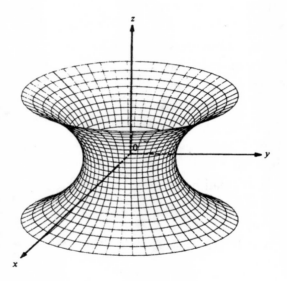

CATENOID

$x(u,v) = (\cosh v \cos u, \cosh v \sin u, v)$ for $\{(u,v); 0 < u < 2\pi, -\infty < v < \infty\}$
A parametric representation of the catenoid

Curved time's monitor,
a page, tubed and squeezed,
no sand falls
through your gentle isometry.
Steam rises,
water of generation
where you mushroom
on the outskirts of cities —
where you mushroom
in a dimly lit room,
the surface between
rib and hip,
new to the hands of a lover
holding
water of generation.

HELICOID

$$x(u,v) = (v \cos u, \ v \sin u, \ cu) \text{ for } \{(u,v); \ 0 < u < 2\pi, \ -\infty < v < \infty\}$$
A parameterization of the helicoid

Archimedes' screw,
you assist the irrigation
of farmers' crops,
as a drill bit,
the construction
of towers.
The arms of a skater in a spin,
auger of a snowblower.
Your flanges support
shelves in a bookcase.
Klaus Barbie's screw,
twisted, you crush a thumb,
suppress a belief,
fulfil a prophecy.

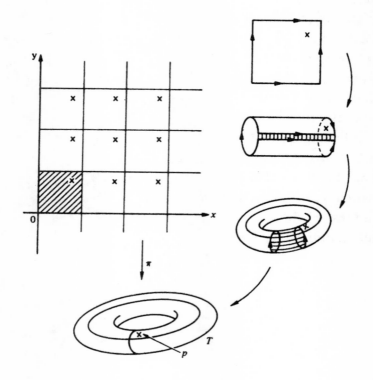

TORUS

$x(u,v) = ((\alpha + \rho \cos(u, v)) \cos v, (\alpha + \rho \cos(u, v)) \sin v, \rho \sin u)$
for $\{(u,v); 0 < u < 2\pi, 0 < v < 2\pi, \alpha > 0, \rho > 0\}$

A parametric representation of the torus

Take this piece of paper.
Identify left and right.
Two sets of circles
generate this particle
accelerator, this doughnut
(cup, steam rising) —
this faulty o-ring in a valve
(brass ring in a bull's nose) —
black tube in a river.
Engorged Ouroborous,
your eyes and mouth
generate this particle
accelerator.
Identify beginning and end.
Take this piece of paper.

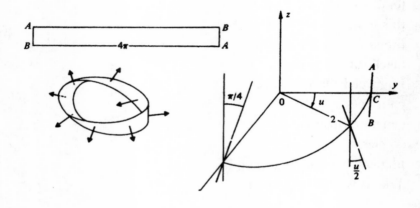

MÖBIUS STRIP

$x(u,v) = ((2 - v \sin \tfrac{1}{2} u) \sin u, (2 - v \sin \tfrac{1}{2} u) \cos u, v \cos \tfrac{1}{2} u),$
for $\{(u,v); 0 < u < 2\pi, -1 < v < 1\}$

A parametric representation of the Möbius strip

O Gétan, I ruin am:
man, I urinate. Go.
You return, upside down,
underneath, facing the same way.
This is a painter's one-stroke paradise,
Escher's ant-walk trellis.
Twist this page.
A difficult trapeze act.
Join the ends.
A clever lover's trap.
In that order.
As wind half-twists a snow-fence.
This boardwalk
in another dimension
cannot be stomped on here.

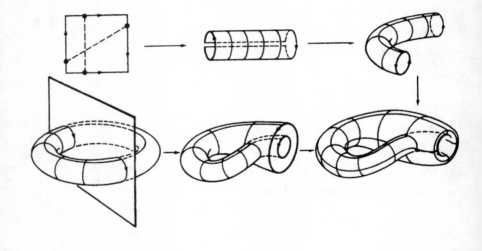

KLEIN BOTTLE

$x(u,v) = ((r \cos v + a) \cos u,\ (r \cos v + a) \sin u,\ r \sin v \cos \frac{1}{2} u,\ r \sin v \sin \frac{1}{2}u)$ for $\{(u,v);\ 0 < u < 2\pi,\ 0 < v < 2\pi\}$

A parameterization of the klein bottle in R^4

Impossible flask,
you can be neither filled
nor emptied —
the lips are dry —
in a desert you collect sunlight,
scorpions gather
bewildered at your boundary.
Your neck enters your side:
a sleeping swan,
a lover alone in a large bed.
You will never be
filled with water.
No one will ever
build a ship in your
impossible flask.

WORMHOLE

Tunnel between worlds
in Einstein's dreams:
the worn drawer-handle
on a writing desk —
a trap — the pipe
collecting water under sinks.
Brass on a deck,
you hold the skiff at dock;
in a hand,
support a coffin.
Centred at a star
no light escapes from,
Einstein dreamed you,
a worm creation.

THE WHOLE: NINE YARNS

1

The six-spoke
water crystal wheel
he calls snowflake
cut with glass

is two three-spoke
water crystal wheels
he calls snow.

One melts on
his tongue.
Two carry his skis,
rise to his knees,
disappear from the road
by the truck load.

2

Rain, rivulet, drop
from sea-steam, lake-steam, river-steam,
cool over hills, fall,
fill reservoir bucket and cup,
pour from bottle and tap
to keep blood thin and flowing.

3

The seed pod wrapped in
organic skin
she calls apple
cored and pared

is flesh and core, now fresh,
soon brown, she calls
to her daughter to share.

In fall, one
rots on the ground.
In spring, spilled
from a split pod,
the seed rises
disguised as roses.

4

Sea-steam carries blue whale semen,
semen of the sea bull
spilled by the surfacing cow.
Sea-steam carries blue whale milk,
milk of the sea cow
spilled by the struggling calf
into unbounded sea.

5

The tall, white cylinder
of water and cellulose fibre
you call lumber
cut along the horizontal

is lumber: two billets share
an edge of identical diameter.
Ninety-seven rings mark
a century of growing bark.

The finest spruce is quarter-
sawn, book-matched for guitar.
Mid-grade pine is two-by-four,
skids of plywood or veneer.
Waste spruce and poplar
mashed with water make paper.

6

Lake-steam carries glacial thaw.
Thaw of forest-covering ice,
faeces of extinct northern birds,
urine of otter and jay,
evaporated pleasure boat oil,
slick of the tanker's spill.

7

The animated shape
near the motionless form
in the street in the fog
called boy

pierced by the nervous sniper,
alert only to motion,
is the motionless form
in the street in the fog
called body

fallen beside his father.
His ululating mother
cambers to his side
unaware that the sniper's suicide
will spare her brother
who runs to help her.

8

Sea-steam carries blue whale blood,
cannon-shot harpoon bursting the lung,
blood of the sea-harvest,
shark-feast of the separated calf,
blood of the sea-birth,
scent of amniotic fluid,
placenta, sea salt.

9

The millions in cities are undistinguished
At a distance. Individuated by scarves, ties
And quality of shoes, they are plucked by the hundred
Every minute from hospitals, collisions, gas stoves,
Group homes, sewer grates, apartments,
Offices, bedrooms, in-ground pools,
Cribs, street corners, and riverbanks to be burned or buried;
The best and worst, footnotes in texts, the rest,
Names passed between generations,
Making way for the two hundred
Born in hospitals, huts, shanties,
Drop in centres, sitting rooms, and clinics
Into the hands of doctors, midwives, fathers,
And mothers, brave and alone.
The new rest unselfconsciously
On their mother's breast
After searching for the nipple
Blindly to see this from a bridge or stars —
Cups of water emptied from a stream
While a spring thunderstorm
Floods the banks of a river that has flowed
As long as memory.